THE
HISTORY
OF
WESTERN
SCULPTURE

A YOUNG PERSON'S GUIDE

JULIET HESLEWOOD

RSVP

RAINTREE
STECK-VAUGHN
PUBLISHERS
The Steck-Vaughn Company

Austin, Texas

Published by Raintree Steck-Vaughn
Publishers, an imprint of Steck-Vaughn
Company

Editors: Jill A. Laidlaw, Shirley Shalit
Designer: Simon Borrough
Picture Researcher: Ann Usborne
Consultant: Susan Wallington

Library of Congress Cataloging-in-Publication Data

Heslewood, Juliet.
    The history of Western sculpture : a young person's
guide / Juliet Heslewood.
        p.   cm.
    Includes bibliographical references and index.
    ISBN 0-8172-4001-2
    1. Sculpture—History.   I. Title.
NB60.H48   1996
730' .9—dc20   95-10247
                                                             CIP
                                                             AC

Typeset by Tom Fenton, Neptune, NJ
Printed in Singapore
Bound in the United States
1 2 3 4 5 6 7 8 9 0 LB 00 99 98 97 96 95

**The back cover picture
is of *Queen Uta* from
Naumburg Cathedral in
Germany (see page 24).**

**Cover pictures, left to
right, Auguste Rodin,
Age of Bronze, 1878
(see page 48), and
Michelangelo's *David*
(see pages 34 and 35).**

For my sister Caggy

Photographic credits

Art and Architecture Collection 7 center, 30 left, 31
above right, 33 bottom right, 34 left and above, 35
right, 45 right, 47 left, 49 above, 50; Bridgeman Art
Library 5, 6 above left, 18, 19 bottom left, 22, 26, 27, 28
left, 29 right, 35 left and center, 36 right, 38 left, 39
bottom, 42 bottom, 46, 48 left, 49 above right, 51 right
and 57 right © ADAGD, Paris, DACS London 1994, 56
© DACS London 1994, 57 left; C. M. Dixon 11 bottom, 12
bottom, 13 bottom, 16 bottom right, 17 left, 24 above, 32
above left; E. T. Archive 6 bottom left, 11 above right, 31
above left and bottom left, 33 bottom left, 34 bottom, 40,
43, 44 above and right; Werner Forman Archive 11
above left, 16 above right and bottom left, courtesy
Galerie Lelong 59 above; Giraudon 45 left, 48 right and
cover; Sonia Halliday Photographs 6 bottom right, 12
center, 13 above and left, 23 bottom; Clive Hicks 17
right, 20 bottom left, 21, 23 left and right, 24 bottom left
and bottom, 25, 32 bottom left; Robert Harding
Associates 19, 30; Michael Holford 7 left, 10, 15 above;
Angelo Hornak 53 right; Life File 54, 55, 58 left;
Popperfoto 55 above; Scala 20 above right, 28 right,
29 left, 33 above, 36 left, 38 right, 39 above, 40, 42 above,
47 right, 51 left, 52 © DACS 1994; Frank Spooner
Pictures 58 bottom; Tate Gallery 53, 57 right, 59 bottom
© Carl Andre/DACS, London/Vaga, New York 1994.

Cover: right Art and Architecture Collection; left
Giraudon; back Clive Hicks.

Contents

Words found in **bold** are explained
in the glossary on pages 60–62.

† Herr John Hacket, being raised
to the Episcopate as 75ᵗʰ Bishop
of Lichfield, a.d. 1661, and finding
this House of God overthrown
by violent and wicked hands, is
impelled by a holy desire to rebuild
that which had been broken down
through his own personal labour

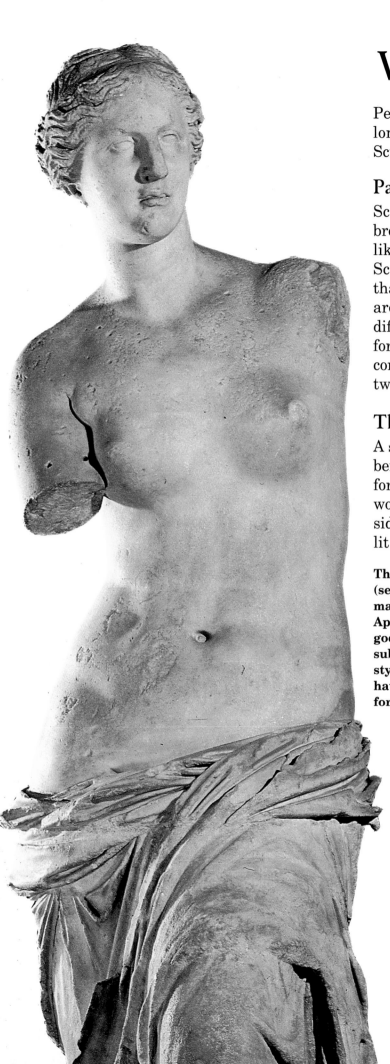

What Is Sculpture?

People have been creating sculpture for as long as human beings have been around. Sculpture is a part of our everyday lives.

Paintings and Sculpture

Sculptors take different materials, such as bronze, marble, or wood, and shape them into likenesses of objects, people, or events. Sculpture is in three dimensions (meaning that it has depth). You can walk all the way around many sculptures and see them from different angles (see pages 24–26 and 34–35 for different views of the same sculptures). In comparison, paintings and drawings are only two dimensional (on a flat surface).

Things to Think About

A sculptor has to ask a great many questions before work can begin. Who is the sculpture for – one person or everybody? Where will the work stand – in a museum, church, inside, outside, or in someone's home? Will it be in a well lit place or a dark place? What should it be

The *Venus de Milo* (see page 7) is a Greek marble statue of Aphrodite, the goddess of love. The subject matter and style of Greek sculpture have influenced artists for centuries.

made out of – stone, cement, bronze, chalk, metal, paper, cardboard, brass, lead, marble, plastic, or glass? Does it have to last for many years in a public place, or only for a short time in one particular exhibition? Will the sculpture be small enough for someone to carry in their pocket or as large as a mountain? Will it be seen close-up or only from a distance? Does the work have to have a serious purpose or can it be made just for fun?

Henry Moore (see page 57) made sculptures out of natural materials in the smooth, curved shapes of natural forms, such as the human figure. This statue is called *Reclining Figure no. 2.*

Taking a Tour of Sculpture

Sculpture is known as one of the fine arts, like painting, music, and writing. Over the centuries, sculptors, painters, musicians, and writers have changed the way their arts look, sound, and read. Sometimes they have had to obey the tastes and choices of the people who **commissioned** their work. But many found new ways of expressing their own ideas. In this book we can take a journey back in time and see the exciting and ever-changing sculptures of the Western world.

1: THE ANCIENT WORLD

Zeus was the chief of all the Greek gods. Bronze statue from Athens, c. 500 B.C. (left).

The Greeks

Greek civilization was well established by about 800 B.C. on the land and islands around the Aegean Sea. The Greek architecture, sculpture, literature, and pottery that have survived tell us much about how the Greeks lived.

The Naked Body

A great deal of Greek sculpture is of nude, or naked, men and women. Nakedness was not unusual for the Greeks. At the Olympic Games, which were founded in Greece in 776 B.C., the athletes wore no clothes so that their performances were unrestricted. The Greeks called a statue of a naked young man a *kouros* and a sculpture of a clothed young woman a *kore*. These statues were usually carved "in the round"–this means that they are not attached to something else, like a wall, but are **free-standing** and carved on all sides. These life-size, stone statues look a bit stiff–they face forward and have one foot slightly ahead of the other. This style of Greek sculpture is called Archaic (c. 650–c. 480 B.C.).

Sculptures that "Move"

As time went on Greek sculptors became more adventurous and tried to depict people in a more natural-looking way. Sculptors looked at the pattern of muscles and the shape of bones under the skin and used their observations to create more lifelike statues. Gradually, these statues showed the human body as more and more perfect, without any faults. This type of figure is known as **ideal** and belongs to the Classical period of Greek sculpture (c. 480–c. 325 B.C.). The term "Classical" originally meant perfectly beautiful.

This *kouros* (c. 540–30 B.C.) stands in the conventional pose. Features of his body like his hair, muscles, and bones are very stylized and not realistic. The lines that have been carved into the marble show general anatomical features. Many ancient sculptures like this one, which is over 2,500 years old, are now preserved in museums (left).

Inspired Sculptures

The naked body could also be sculpted to express great emotions like fear, pain, and love. The later Hellenistic style of Greek sculpture (c. 323–27 B.C.) emphasizes people's emotions. One of the most famous sculptures of this period is *Laocoön* (second century B.C. to first century A.D.). The **Trojan** priest Laocoön and his sons were crushed to death by sea snakes sent by the god **Apollo.** Laocoön looks as though he is just about to succumb to the snakes that will eventually kill him.

Venus de Milo **(c. 100 B.C.) seems relaxed as she leans on one leg, her clothes falling away from her.**

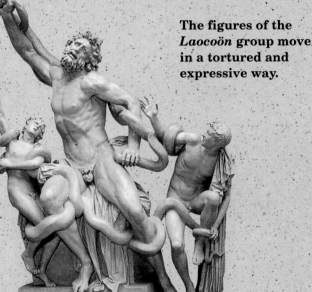

The figures of the *Laocoön* **group move in a tortured and expressive way.**

Marble is still found in the same quarries today but it is moved with modern machinery and transportation. This is the Carrara marble quarry in Italy.

Marble

Marble is a stone of many different colors. Often sculptors use white marble (like the Greeks), because of its fresh, pure appearance and the sparkling shine to which it can be polished. Marble is cut in large blocks from quarries. From the earliest times marble has been cut out of the quarry and dragged away by animals. Because of its weight and the difficulty of moving it from one place to another the rough shape and size of the statue may already have been decided by the sculptor before he or she began to carve it.

7

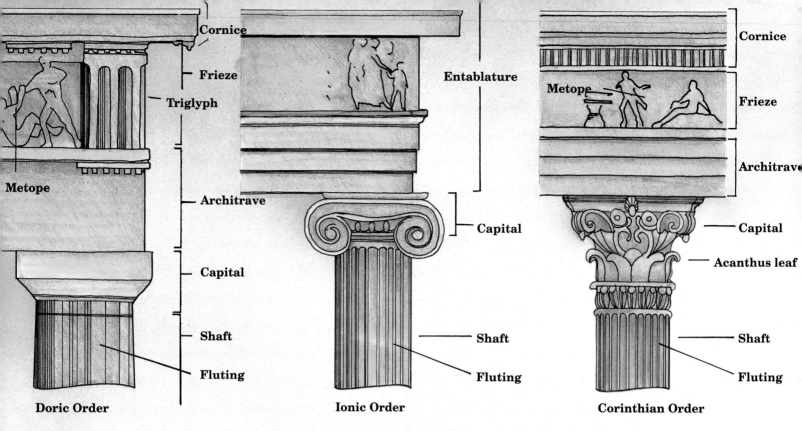

Cornice

Frieze

Triglyph

Metope

Architrave

Capital

Shaft

Fluting

Doric Order

Entablature

Metope

Capital

Shaft

Fluting

Ionic Order

Cornice

Frieze

Architrave

Capital

Acanthus leaf

Shaft

Fluting

Corinthian Order

Greek Temples

Temple Sculptures

The temple was one of the most important buildings in a Greek town. Here people worshipped their gods. Temples were rectangular, with columns holding up the roof over an entrance and **sanctuary.** In the sanctuary stood a **colossal** statue of the god to whom the temple was **dedicated.** Many different sculptures were incorporated into the architecture of the temple as decoration. The sculptures were named according to the architectural shape they fitted into.

Parts of a Temple

At each end of the temple was a triangular block of stone called a pediment that helped to hold up the roof. Figures would stand, sit, or lie down to fit its shape. Running continuously around the top of the four walls was a story told in sculpture relating to the god of the temple. This **frieze** was made up of alternating blocks of stone – a plain stone decorated with vertical grooves (called a triglyph) followed by a stone decorated with the next scene of the story (called a metope).

Different styles of Greek architecture were named according to the type of column used. The columns varied depending on the type of carving at the top (called the capital) and the number of flutes (grooves) in the column (called the shaft).

A Greek temple (bottom) was made up of many architectural and sculptural features. Some of these features are still used today and are still known by the same names.

8

High and Low Relief

A block of stone that is only cut on one side is called a relief. The frieze of the temple was usually carved in this way but there were two different methods that could be used. When the sculptor carves the image deeply into the stone it is known as high relief. When the image is lightly cut into the stone it is called low relief. Skilled sculptors had to be aware of the different effects that these **techniques** could create and also how sunlight and candlelight could change the appearance of the shapes they had carved.

This is a metope from the frieze of the Parthenon.

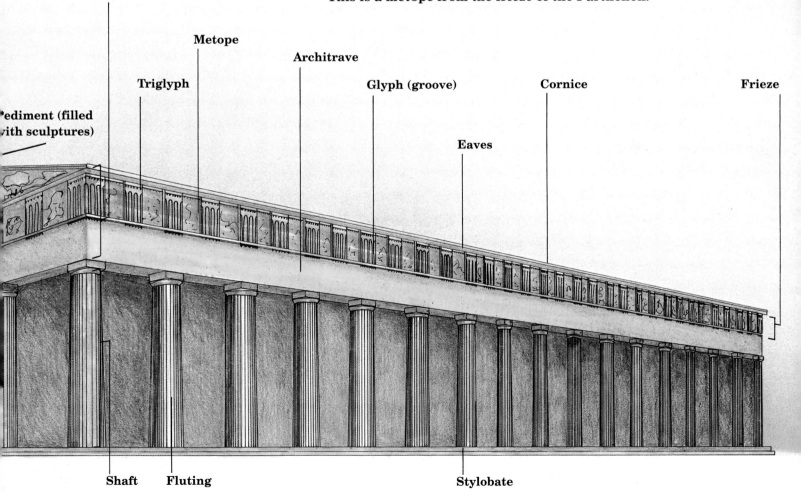

Entablature

Metope

Triglyph

Architrave

Glyph (groove)

Cornice

Frieze

Pediment (filled with sculptures)

Eaves

Shaft   Fluting

Stylobate

Roman Faces

The Romans

Northwest of Greece, in Italy, a new power was gaining control over the whole of the **Mediterranean.** By the second century B.C. Rome had grown from a small town into the center of an expanding empire. Greece and other countries as far away as the north of Europe and Africa all came under Roman control. In 27 B.C. the Roman Empire was established under Emperor Augustus and a time of peace followed. Although the Romans collected, copied, and admired Greek art they also created sculpture to suit their own needs.

The Emperor

What kind of man could rule an enormous empire? In those days, when there were no cameras, newspapers, or televisions, not many people knew what the emperor looked like. In the statues that were made of him he always looked strong, fit, and valiant – even if he wasn't. A sculpted **bust** of the emperor could be reproduced in thousands of copies. In a quiet corner inside the home of a rich Roman, the emperor's sculpted head glowed from the light of a candle placed in front of it. This was rather like having a picture of a king or a president on the wall.

Citizens and Countrymen

An emperor was always made to look glorious in any form of art. But other people were also thought of as important in Roman art. Between 13 and 9 B.C. the *Ara Pacis* or the *Peace Altar* was made for Emperor Augustus Caesar. The altar had a sculpted frieze (in high relief) and panels decorated with a leaf design. As well as Augustus and his family, you can see the sculpted figures of **magistrates, senators,** religious leaders, and small children walking in a procession. Everyone in the frieze looks natural, as if we are seeing exactly how they would appear on the day the altar was dedicated.

This Greek head is of an unknown goddess. Her features were imagined and sculpted in an "ideal" way. The Romans imitated the Greek style of sculpture. Second to first centuries B.C.

This huge head is part of a complete statue of the Roman emperor *Constantine*, most of which is now missing. Its huge size impressed people with the emperor's power.
Constantine, early fourth century A.D.

This portrait bust gives us a good idea of how the Roman emperor Vespasian looked. His interesting features and expression are not idealized but are realistic (dates unknown).

Private Sculptures

When wealthy people gathered together because of a death in the family they carried wax masks or busts of their ancestors with them to the funeral. The Romans were more interested than the Greeks in making sculptures that were exact likenesses of people, and so Roman faces are mostly **realistic** while Greek portraits tend to be idealized.

These Roman citizens are portrayed on the *Ara Pacis*. This altar commemorated the conquest of Spain and Gaul by Augustus in 13 B.C. and the peace in the empire that followed.

11

Stories in Stone

Wars and soldiers, victories and conquest – the Romans were used to winning battles throughout their empire. For over five hundred years their power spread and they created sculptures that celebrated their success.

The Triumphal Arch

It was the Romans who first thought of turning an arch into a **commemorative** work of art. Arches were used as gateways to cities or placed at junctions on the many roads the Romans built across the empire. Different parts of the arch were decorated with columns, friezes, statues, and panels. The arch was often used as the base for a larger statue of the emperor on horseback or riding a chariot. A large inscription, boldly written in **Latin,** explained who or what the arch commemorated or celebrated.

The Triumphal Column

Single, freestanding, tall columns were built up block by block rather like a wall or a building. These columns were covered in battle scenes sculpted in both high and low relief. Great attention was paid to telling the story of the battle. Like a scroll, the carved pictures wound their way up the column to meet a statue placed at the top. Unlike arches, columns usually celebrated a particular person such as a soldier who had led a successful army.

Trajan's Column

Trajan's Column (dedicated A.D. 114) in Rome is almost a hundred feet tall with six hundred and fifty feet of carved reliefs spiraling around it. So that the story could be easily understood from the ground, the heads and shoulders of the figures were often carved in higher relief than other details. The whole column was painted to help the story stand out even more, just as in Greek temple sculptures (see pages 8–9).

The Roman emperor Titus is seen here returning from Jerusalem.
Arch of Titus, A.D. 81.

Hide and Seek

Jesus Christ was born in the time of the Romans. At first, people who believed in him were **persecuted.** Christ's followers had to pray in secret and their images of Jesus had to be disguised. Many **symbols** were created to hide Christian meanings –a carved relief of a shepherd and a lamb was a way of showing Christ with his flock of followers.

If you stand close to *Trajan's Column* (left), you can read the stories that spiral upward. The carvings at the top (below left) cannot be read from ground level.

The Arch of Titus can still be seen in Rome.

Modern letters are based on Roman inscriptions, (background).

13

Bronze

Bronze is the name given to a mixture of metals – usually copper, lead, and **zinc** – that contains no iron. During the centuries before the birth of Christ bronze was one of the most useful materials for making sculptures. Bronze is hard, long-lasting, and unlike stone will not easily chip or break.

These photographs show a sculpture going through stages of modern bronze casting. Very little has changed since ancient times.

Casting

There are a few ways of casting a statue in bronze. The most common way is called the lost wax method (see photographs below). First a model is made out of a fireproof material like clay. The clay is then covered with wax. Another layer of fireproof clay is applied on top of the wax. A mold has now been created. The mold is heated to a high temperature until the wax melts and can be poured away. In place of the wax goes hot, liquid bronze. When it is cool the bronze becomes very hard. The sculpture inside the mold is now ready to be revealed once all the clay has been chipped away.

The sculptor's model.

Soft clay is placed over half of the model and plaster is then poured over it. The plaster is left to harden. This process is repeated on the other half.

The clay is removed from the plaster mold and the two halves are joined together. Molten rubber is poured into the mold and hardens.

The model is removed from the rubber mold. The two halves are joined again and liquid wax is poured into the mold and hardens.

The two halves of the mold are separated.

The wax replica of the original model is now removed from the mold.

Dipping the wax into a ceramic (pottery) solution is the next stage. This happens twice.

The ceramic shell is left to harden, before it is placed in an oven where the heat melts the wax.

Shining

Bronze can be polished to a brilliant shine. When the statue is freed from its mold it usually has all sorts of rough surfaces on it. The sculptor smooths these down with a file. The next stage is to rub an **abrasive,** such as sand or a **pumice stone,** against the bronze to carefully grind away the uneven parts. A metal's shine is far brighter than the sparkling effect of marble.

Horses and Riders

Bronze is the finest material for **equestrian** statues. A horse and its rider are a difficult subject to balance correctly – the horse's thin legs need to support both its own weight and the weight of the rider. In real life this is possible but in sculpture the material needs to do the work of weight-bearing muscles and bones. Stone breaks under this strain but bronze is strong and because the statue is hollow there is not as much weight on the horse's legs.

Bronze allowed sculptors to create large statues that would survive all weathers. *Marcus Aurelius,* completed c. A.D. 80.

The hollow shell is packed in sand and molten bronze is poured into it – a difficult and dangerous operation. This is left to cool.

After the ceramic shell has been chipped off the bronze can be polished or colored to a bright shine.

15

2 : THE MIDDLE AGES

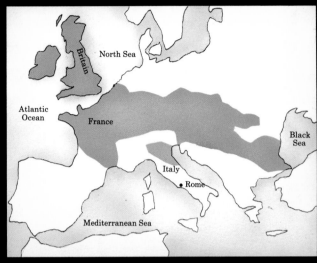

Celtic tribes (along with many others) moved across Europe over hundreds of years. This map shows how far they traveled.

The Celts were very talented craftsmen. They created intricate and decorative patterns in bronze and other metals. *Circular Harness Plaque*, fifth century B.C.

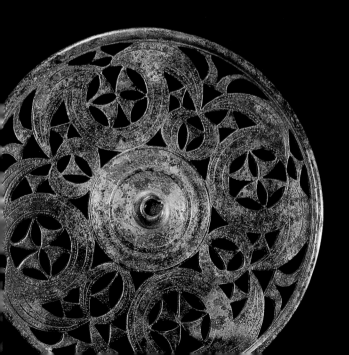

The Celts

The Roman Empire gradually began to lose its power as the **Barbarians** advanced across Europe. By A.D. 476 the Roman Empire as it used to be no longer existed and the time we call the Middle Ages (fifth–fifteenth centuries) followed.

The Celts were an **Iron Age** people who spread across Europe in the sixth and fifth centuries B.C. (see map). These people were practically wiped out by the Roman Empire but managed to survive in places like Brittany (France), the Hebrides (Scotland), Ireland, and Wales. Celtic art and culture had a kind of **renaissance** (see pages 26–35) during the Middle Ages from about 400–1200.

Everyday objects, including jewelry, were always highly decorated. *Tubular gold torque*, Ireland, first century B.C.

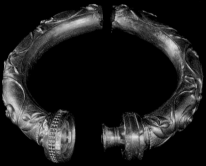

A Natural Style

The world of nature gave the Celts many ideas for their art. Figures of animals were carved on eating and drinking vessels, jewelry, and weapons. Plants provided interesting shapes, swirls, and knots. The Celts did not copy nature exactly, but turned natural forms into a **formal** style of art.

Many of the pieces of Celtic art that have survived are made of metals like bronze (see pages 14–15) or silver. Most of these objects are small and were intended to be useful in everyday life – in the home, on the hunt, or in fighting. Small stone statues represent Celtic gods such as Cernunnos who had three heads. Wood was available in large quantities but the objects that were made of it have not survived.

The Christian Cross

Christianity began to spread from Ireland to the British Isles after about A.D. 461. More monasteries were built and Celtic art gradually changed to include Christian images. The cross is the symbol of Christ's crucifixion and is a very important part of this Celtic and Christian art.

A circular shape inside a cross is a typical Celtic design.
Cross of Scriptures, **Clonmacnois, Ireland, ninth-tenth centuries.**

The earliest crosses were sculpted out of large blocks of stone. These stones were carved lightly, as if the images had just been drawn on. As time went on this style changed and the designs were deeply carved in high relief. The decoration on crosses became much more elaborate, with interlacing patterns, symbols, and figures from the Bible.

A ninth century carving showing two scenes from the Bible: *The Flight into Egypt, Loaves and Fishes.*

An eighth century *Crucifixion* **scene from Ireland (left).**

17

Charlemagne's Books

Charlemagne was the ruler of the Franks, a group of Germanic tribes that conquered what we now call France, Germany, and Austria. When he was crowned emperor he was thought to be as great as any Ancient Roman emperor. Art of his reign is called Carolingian.

This illustration comes from a manuscript called the *Kings of France*. It was painted seven centuries after Charlemagne lived and shows his army at war with the Trojans (left).

Libraries

Charlemagne loved books. He believed th[at] education and schools were important [for] people of all ages and he brought many teach[ers] to attend his court. Despite his enthusiasm [for] education, Charlemagne found writing di[ffi]cult. But it was during his reign (766–814) th[at] writing took on a new look. At this time peo[ple] wrote everything in capitals, or upperca[se] letters. During Charlemagne's time small, lowercase, letters were introduced.

Charlemagne spoke German but he believ[ed] that Latin should be used for official or re[li]gious purposes. In the monasteries mon[ks] copied ancient texts and gradually, fabul[ous] libraries were created. Each book contain[ed] beautiful hand-painted pictures, called illu[mi]nations, that decorated the pages.

Ivory

These precious books needed equally beauti[ful] covers. The cover had to be protective, ha[rd] wearing and related to the subject of the bo[ok]. Many materials were useful for the covers [of] books – wood, gold, beaten metal, jewe[ls,] leather, and ivory. All of these materials cou[ld] be used to make small, perfect, **portab[le]** sculptures on the covers.

Ivory is made from animal tusks (teet[h,] usually from elephants. Charlemagne's emp[ire] traded with many foreign countries – [his] messengers went as far as India and Chi[na] on both land and sea. The king of the **Persia[ns]** once sent Charlemagne an elephant as [a] present – so ivory was familiar in his court.

A large tusk could be almost seven inch[es] in **diameter,** so an ivory sculpture could [be] no bigger than this. Ivory was perfect [for] small objects and especially for finely-carv[ed] book covers. Ivory is very hard and its pa[le] surface can be polished to a **translucent** fini[sh]. During Charlemagne's time ivory book cove[rs] became very popular. At first simple designs [of] figures surrounded by **lacework** patter[ns] were carved. Later these tiny sculptures we[re] encrusted with gold and jewels.

Books were often covered with carved ivory. *Ivory Prayer Book Cover*, Carolingian (left, right, and title page).

Elephants were hunte[d] for their tusks. Today, elephants are protecte[d] animals (main picture right).

18

The Romanesque

In the first century A.D. Christian churches were just like auditoriums. By the sixth century they had become a circular shape, and by the tenth century churches had become the cross shape we are familiar with today. Certain parts of a church were decorated with sculpture—such as the tympanum and the capitals (see boxes). These sculptures were made according to the fashion of the time. By the middle of the eleventh century a particular type of sculpture had developed which we now call Romanesque because it looks very much like Ancient Roman architecture and sculpture.

Sculptures for the Church

Europe became calmer than it had been since the fall of the Roman Empire and people felt a new confidence during the eleventh century. Up until this point in the Middle Ages, sculpture had been on a small scale, carved lightly in relief onto book covers or on portable objects. But with the building of greater, more impressive churches and cathedrals, sculptors began carving huge intricate works as a part of the grand architecture.

The Pilgrim Roads

Some of the finest Romanesque sculptures are to be found in southwestern France and northern Spain. At this time people went on **pilgrimages** to various cathedrals that housed the remains of saints. The pilgrim road to Santiago de Compostela in northern Spain was one of the most popular pilgrimage

This tympanum from Bourges Cathedral (France) shows clearly the influence of Roman and Romanesque storytelling in stone.

The Tympanum

The people who attended church did not always know how to read or write. As they entered a church porch they looked up at its tympanum—the semicircular area above the main door. Here were carved important scenes from the Bible, like the *Last Judgment*. All the parts of the story had to be arranged into a **composition** that would fit inside the tympanum's shape. Christ, Mary, the apostles, angels, devils—all these characters needed to be clear and easily seen. The size of the figures changed according to their importance—for instance, Christ was always larger than any other figure.

Sculptors often had a sense of humor. This figure peeps from one of the arches surrounding the tympanum at anyone coming into Conques Cathedral (France, c. 1050–1130).

routes. All along the roads to this cathedral, churches were richly covered with sculptures telling the Christian story and offering the pilgrims a place to pray. These sculptures were large, dramatic, and more powerful than the illuminated manuscripts and small paintings that only monks had been able to see for the past couple of hundred years. They were made for ordinary people to pray at and some showed bloodthirsty dramas depicting the awful torments of hell.

Grotesque figures and monsters were included in church sculptures to remind people of hell (below). Chauvigny Cathedral (France), begun after 1100, *Capital* in the apse.

Capitals

The top of a column or pilaster did not go straight into the curve of an arch but was decorated with sculptures on every side. This is called a capital. Separate scenes from the Bible were shown, or a grotesque–a very ugly face that was meant to be a horrible warning against the temptations of the devil. There was only a limited amount of space on a capital so the top of the column was often covered with carved plants.

Many architectural features were decorated with simple designs, plants, figures, or heads (right). *Capital* from Aulnay Cathedral (France), twelfth century.

From Stonemason
to Sculptor

**During the construction of a cathedral, many
people came to watch its progress.**
Building of a Cathedral, Jean Fouquet (c. 1420–81).

During the Middle Ages hundreds of churches were constructed across Europe, and thousands of people found work building them. The jobs of architect, **mason,** and sculptor were all closely linked. Churches and abbeys could take from ten to two hundred years to be completed, depending on their size. Money was needed to pay for these buildings and this often came from local taxes or gifts. The *Tour de Beurre (Butter Tower)* in Rouen (France) was paid for by people who bought permission to eat butter during **Lent.**

The Building Site

The design of a building and the sculptures on a building were usually the work of a **master-mason.** If it was to be a palace or castle, the **patron,** or owner would explain what was wanted. The master-mason inspected the stone in the quarry and this was brought to the site by river (as far as possible). The master-mason organized a team of workers and helped to teach unskilled masons who might not have had much experience. Other masons practiced laying stone walls and finishing the building's final appearance. A **lodge,** like a hut, provided shelter for the workmen and their tools and also served as a place to eat and rest. The masons sometimes cut and shaped the stones inside the lodge. These craftsmen were the sculptors of the time.

This part of the tympanum at Autun Cathedral by Gislebertus, shows people who have been sent to hell (above, across both pages).

This stained glass detail (below) from Lichfield Cathedral (England) shows a stonemason at work.

† Here John Hacket, being raised to the Episcopate as 75th Bishop of Lichfield, a.d.1661, and finding this House of God overthrown by violent and wicked hands, is impelled by a holy desire to rebuild that which had been broken down through his own personal labour and munificence, as well as by the offering of the faithful he

Image-Makers

Masons carved figures out of stone. Those who were very good at this became known as image-makers. The stone was often hoisted into position on the building and then was carved. But as buildings grew higher, image-making more complicated, and the designs more difficult to handle, the blocks of stone were more likely to stay on the ground and shapes were chalked onto them to show the mason where to carve.

Some image-makers became well known for their work. Some even signed their names in the stone, like Gislebertus (dates unknown) on the tympanum at Autun Cathedral in France (c. 1130–35). As a mason traveled from town to town practicing his craft, so his fame spread. In this way, the mason gradually became known as a sculptor and an artist.

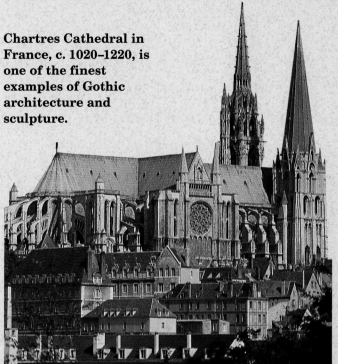

Chartres Cathedral in France, c. 1020–1220, is one of the finest examples of Gothic architecture and sculpture.

The Gothic

During the Middle Ages, the church was the center of a village or town and other buildings grew up around it. The church was **symbolic** of God's divine power. Kings and noblemen ruled in the cities and the country, but it was religion that most strongly affected everybody's lives.

Sculpture Spreads

In France, the great cathedrals soared to over 100 feet in height. Every available space on the cathedral was now filled with sculptures. Arches, windows, and doorways had become pointed rather than round. The shapes of the buildings were finished off with richly carved, detailed sculptures. Sculptors came from all over Europe to train in the famous cathedral workshops of France.

This lovely statue of *Queen Uta* is attached to the wall of the choir of Naumburg Cathedral in Germany, c. 1260.

Naturalism

Sculpted Romanesque figures (see pages 20–21) stand stiffly upright, making you very aware that they are fixed to the wall. By the middle of the thirteenth century sculptures began to look more realistic. Sculptures of the Virgin Mary and Jesus seem to bend and sway rather than just stand in rigid positions. This more relaxed style is called Gothic. Flowers and plants were copied and used time and time again as a way of filling in or linking together different bits of architecture. Sculptures of the natural world were very popular with church-goers because nature is an important part of God's creation in the Christian religion.

Some sculptures at the doors of cathedrals are almost "in the round" and can be seen from several angles. Chartres Cathedral, *Apostle*, thirteenth century.

Gothic masons were expert at handling stone. Large expanses of wall-space, like this one at Reims Cathedral in France (left), were covered with details. Twelfth century.

3: THE RENAISSANCE

The figures on Nicola Pisano's pulpit in the baptistery next to Pisa Cathedral in Italy neatly fit around its shape, 1260.

Giovanni Pisano's pulpit in Pisa Cathedral has many more figures than Nicola's carved into it, c. 1315.

Italy

In Italy, reminders of Ancient Roman culture were never far away. Italians went to Rome to look at what was left of the architecture and sculpture of the empire. Sculptors studied Roman artists and copied their work.

The Renaissance blossomed in Italy during the fifteenth century. The name Renaissance comes from a French word meaning "rebirth." Competition between artists grew as they tried to reproduce the world more and more realistically in paintings and sculptures. A new type of art soon dominated Europe.

Pulpits from Pisa

Nicola Pisano (c. 1220–1284), as his name tells us, came from Pisa, which is about one hundred ninety miles from Rome. In his hometown he made a **pulpit** (1260) for the town's **baptistery** in the shape of a hexagon (with six sides). This

sculpture reveals how much he admired and imitated Roman art. One of the figures that separate the panels on this pulpit is very like a figure from a Roman **sarcophagus** that Nicola would have seen in Pisa. Five years later Nicola made a pulpit in Pisa for Siena Cathedral. This time it was octagonal (with eight sides). Here, the scenes inside the panels are much more crowded with figures spilling out toward each other.

Nicola's son, Giovanni Pisano (c. 1250–1320) also became a sculptor. He made two pulpits and his panels are even more lively and dramatic than his father's.

Sculptors took the things that they admired from the art around them and learned from the masters of the past. For another century, Gothic and Ancient Roman art were combined to form a constantly changing style.

26

Ghiberti's winning panel, *The Sacrifice of Isaac*, from the baptistery doors in Florence.

A Competition

In 1401, a competition was announced in Florence, a town not far from Pisa. Sculptors were asked to make a single bronze panel depicting *The Sacrifice of Isaac* (above). This panel would serve as an example for a whole set of door panels for the Florentine baptistery. Bronze casting was not popular in Florence and the two finalists were goldsmiths. The difficulty was how to fit a scene from the Bible into the odd quatrefoil shape of the panel (see above). The winner of the competition, Lorenzo Ghiberti (1378–1455), divided the scene up with a mass of rock. One side of the picture is full of action and the other is calm and peaceful. Ghiberti combined effects that had been perfected by the Romans, like the twisting, naked body of Isaac with Gothic details like swirling clothes and natural-looking animals and faces.

Donatello

Artists and sculptors benefited from Italy's new-found prosperity because they were paid to produce more and more work. Donatello (c. 1385/6–1466) was apprenticed to Ghiberti (see previous page) in Florence at this time but his sculptures are totally different from his teacher's.

Donatello's youthful figure of *David* calmly stands with Goliath's head at his feet, c. 1430–32.

Drawing Reliefs

Donatello was interested in the laws of perspective that were frequently discussed and illustrated at this time. Perspective is the name given to the drawing technique that allows artists to show the way objects recede into the distance in painting, drawing, and relief sculpture. Looking inside Donatello's almost flat relief scenes you are fooled and imagine that you can see a world of depth where there is none. There are clues as to how Donatello did this in the tiny details of his work – the lines of tiles on a floor, the small distant hills, the gradually disappearing walls of a building. He lightly **incised** the marble as if he were using a pen on paper, not a chisel on marble. Areas of low and high relief merge into each other like drawings of light and shade. Donatello's bronze reliefs show how he used his knowledge of drawing and casting to make powerful sculptures.

Saints and Prophets

Stories from the Bible have been depicted over and over again in Western sculpture. Sometimes these characters and stories look similar because sculptors copy each others' works. When Donatello made statues of saints and **prophets** he decided to give each one a distinct and individual character so that they would look like real people. Donatello's *Saint George* (c. 1415–17) stands unafraid and ready to fight from his **niche** of the church of Orsanmichele in Florence. High up on the walls of Florence Cathedral, Donatello's freestanding figures of prophets look down onto the street. Their serious and sturdy heads, arms, and hands remind you of the importance of the Christian message. Donatello appreciated the value of the stone's weight and emphasized this in the massive gowns of the prophets that fix each one firmly into his niche. Donatello always thought about where his statues would stand and how they would be looked at and understood – as works of art and also as respected figures from the Bible.

Donatello made the Old Testament prophet *Abacuc* look down thoughtfully from the top of Forence Cathedral, c. 1411–36.

Below the striking figure of *St. George*, Donatello included a relief that shows the saint slaying the dragon.

29

Florence

Italy was a land often troubled by wars between its states. These **city-states** were ruled by rich and successful families who had a great deal of money to spend on arms, a rich lifestyle, palaces, and art. They chose the finest artists to make their homes and towns as beautiful as possible. Florence was a wealthy city because of its international trade in cloth. The powerful families who lived there were determined to compete with each other over the art that would reflect their power. It was through art that they wanted to be remembered for centuries to come.

Florentine Families

Some of the most famous families in Florence — the **Medici,** the Pazzi, the Strozzi — are still remembered today. Together with other families' names, they can be found on portraits, on memorials, in chapels, and on public monuments. Artists had to keep pace with their patrons' demands as well as keeping "in fashion." When Donatello left Florence in 1443 to work for ten years in the city of Padua, the sculptors that were left behind developed a different style.

The members of the Medici family were shown in paintings, sculptures, and coins. *Cosimo de' Medici* **(top of page).**

The dome of Florence Cathedral still dominates the skyline of the city.

A "soft" style of marble-carving was very popular with wealthy patrons.
Cosimo de' Medici and Family, Giovanni Antonio de Rossi, 1517–75.

Color glazes helped to highlight images and details carved in terra-cotta (below). *Madonna and Child,* Andrea Della Robbia (1435–1525).

Training Sculptors

The work that sculptors now had to do was not something that could be learned on a building site. Besides learning from Ancient Roman sculpture, artists needed to learn more practical lessons from "masters." A master was someone who was successful and recognized for his art.

With a great deal of work to produce, a master had a large studio or workshop. Apprentice sculptors would help the master on a commission he had been given – perhaps doing the rough cutting of a statue. Pupils also helped generally with the preparation of clay and the care of materials and tools. In return a young apprentice learned all the skills needed to become a sculptor.

The Garden of Lorenzo de' Medici by Giovanni da Sangiovanni, 1592–1636.

Northern Europe

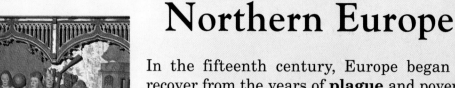

In the fifteenth century, Europe began to recover from the years of **plague** and poverty that had killed thousands of people the century before. Life was improved by the trade that was growing between countries. While in Italy new thoughts and discoveries led to the "rebirth" that was the Renaissance, Northern Europe made its own artistic progress.

Realism

Looking at nature and copying its details was a familiar part of the Gothic sculptor's work. Northern sculptors adapted the Gothic style into a forceful way of looking at the world around them. This is called realism and it is the opposite of idealism (see pages 6–7 and 10–11). To be realistic is to depict the truth, even if it is ugly.

Sculpting Real People?

The **Netherlandish** sculptor Claus Sluter (died 1406) made a large fountain for a monastery near Dijon in France called the *Well of Moses* (1395–1406). Only the base of this fountain has survived intact. Figures of **Old Testament** prophets stand around its base— they are just as impressive as Donatello's prophets (see page 29) and yet they were made twenty years earlier. The faces look so real that they might be portraits of real people—one even wore specially made copper spectacles!

Wood and Stone

Veit Stoss (1450–1533) specialized in wood carving, as did many northern sculptors. Stoss's figures look very posed, as if they have been standing still for far too long. Their gestures are stiff, bold, and powerful.

Tilman Riemenschneider (c. 1460–1531) was very popular in Germany where he had a large workshop. You can recognize his realism in the heads of his figures, which are very angular and surrounded by thick coils of hair.

Although these people have been sent to hell, they have taken their hats with them, which show us their professions. *Hell's Mouth* from *The Last Judgment*, Sweden, c. 1400, sculptor unknown.

Claus Sluter shows *Moses* to be a wise old prophet looking out from a symbolic well at the cloister of the Charterhouse of Champmol, Dijon, France (left). Detail from *The Well of Moses*, 1395–1406.

Wood

Wood is a very changeable material. When a tree is cut down it is said to be "green" or new. Wood alters shape depending on how it is dried. Most wood is dried outside and this can take from eighteen months to six years, depending on the type of wood. Once dry, wood is lighter and unlikely to change shape. The patterns running through wood can be useful for decorative effects in sculpture. Wood does not chip like stone and can be carved in very fine detail. Wood was often painted after its surface had been prepared with a special **ground.** Polished wood has a warm glow unlike the brilliance of bronze or the translucent light of marble. Wood needs to be

The *Madonna and Child* was a very popular subject in both painting and sculpture. Veit Stoss, c. 1477–92, Nuremburg Cathedral.

We know this figure is a churchman from his clothing and the fact that he is leaning on the Bible. *Choir of St. Stephen's Cathedral*, Vienna, Anton Pilgram, sixteenth century.

By 1525, when this wooden *Lamentation* was carved, the influence of Italian art could be seen in the North. Artist unknown.

painted with a final protective coat or it may change color when it is exposed to light, rather like an old photograph fading. It can also decay because of mold or wood-eating insects and woodworms. Over the centuries, varnishes have changed from mixtures of egg and oil to **synthetic** substances.

Michelangelo

As the fifteenth century came to an end, after great achievements in art, Florence produced Michelangelo Buonarotti (1475–1564), an artist, architect, and sculptor who was hailed as a **genius.**

Michelangelo painted himself among the figures on the *Sistine Chapel Ceiling,* 1508–12.

Michelangelo's Patrons

When his colossal statue *David* was erected in the center of Florence, Michelangelo became instantly famous. While still young, he was sought after by the most influential patrons in Italy. In 1505 Pope Julius II called him to Rome to design his tomb. Michelangelo worked on this project for fifteen years and yet it was never completed. The two men often quarreled and plans for the tomb kept changing as Michelangelo was asked to do other work—including the painting of the *Sistine Chapel Ceiling.* In Florence, the Medici family asked Michelangelo to design buildings as well as their own tombs.

Body and Soul

Michelangelo went to the quarries to choose his marble himself. Michelangelo believed that statues were imprisoned inside the marble and that the sculptor had to labor to release the image. Although Michelanglo's statues were carved "in the round" (see page 6) he started sculpting from only one side as if it were a relief. In this way he began to free his imagined image, cutting away the stone and watching it appear to the world.

Most of Michelangelo's statues are of bold, muscular bodies that seem to move in a way that is almost unnatural but full of power. In 1506, the statue of *Laocoön* (see pages 6–7) was discovered under a vineyard in Rome. Michelangelo rushed to the site to see the statue come

Michelangelo's *David* pauses and thinks before he moves to slay the giant, 1501–04.

out of the ground. Michelangelo did not just copy this brilliant Greek sculpture, he seemed to compete with it. His figures, even when unfinished, show people expressing powerful emotions.

This figure of *Moses*, c. 1513–15, is one of the few that finally appeared on the *Tomb of Julius II*, c. 1503–c. 1513 (left).

Plans for the *Tomb of Julius II* were altered many times and the work was never finished as Michelangelo wanted it originally. Julius can be seen lying down above *Moses*.

***St. Matthew* appears to be reaching out of the stone to release himself, 1505–06.**

35

4: CHURCH AND STATE

Myths and Manners

Sculptors of the late sixteenth century were often compared with Michelangelo. Many of them didn't copy his style exactly, but borrowed his ideas and adapted them for their own purposes, rather as the Romans had learned from Greek sculpture (see pages 10–11). Michelangelo had carved twisting and turning figures that were admired by private patrons and the Church. The sculptors of the sixteenth century exaggerated Michelangelo's style and made sculptures of people with graceful, spiraling bodies and long arms and legs. This style of drawing, painting, and sculpting is called Mannerism.

Perseus (left), like Donatello's *David* (see page 28), is triumphant yet calm in victory. Benevenuto Cellini, *Perseus*, 1545–54.

This saltcellar is the only work by Cellini in gold that has survived. The male figure represents the sea and he guards the boat-shaped salt holder with his spear. The female figure represents the earth, where pepper comes from, and she is seated next to the pepper container. *Saltcellar of Francis I*, 1539–43.

Benvenuto Cellini

Benvenuto Cellini (1500–71) was a Florentine goldsmith and sculptor. In his autobiography (first published in 1728) he wrote about his life and art and declared that sculpture was a more difficult skill than painting because a statue has more than one side. When you look at a painting you instantly see the whole picture but you can walk around a sculpture and see it from many different angles.

Cellini worked for King Francis I of France from 1540–45, and also for the Medici family in Florence (1545–71). Cosimo de' Medici asked Cellini to sculpt his masterpiece – a large bronze image of the Greek god **Perseus** (1545–54). Perseus (opposite page) is shown holding the head of **Medusa** whose newly-killed body lies around his feet.

Giovanni Bologna

Giovanni Bologna (1529–1608) was a Frenchman who was influenced by Michelangelo's work. Giovanni met Michelangelo when he traveled to Italy in 1555. Michelangelo's figures were always the same size as their blocks of marble but Giovanni wanted his figures to reach out into the space around them. In order to make this possible Giovanni added separate pieces of stone to the original block.

For centuries, sculptors had been trying to find different ways to carve two figures balancing on a small base. Giovanni stunned the people of Florence when he completed *The Rape of the Sabine Woman* in 1583 (see right). Giovanni managed to sculpt not two but three people all reaching upward from a restricted space as if they were all caught inside an invisible cylinder.

Making Models

When planning different aspects of a statue, sculptors made a small-scale model or *bozzetto* (which means sketch or model in Italian). These bozzettos are usually made of clay or wax. Models can be held easily and looked at from every angle to give an idea of how the large-scale statue will look.

Some of the most famous pieces of Florentine sculpture can be seen in the Loggia dei Lanzi in Florence, including Giovanni Bologna's *The Rape of the Sabine Woman* (right), 1579–83.

37

Bernini

Gianlorenzo Bernini (1598–1680) was the son of an Italian sculptor and he became an expert sculptor while he was still very young. Bernini's patrons included popes, princes, cardinals, and dukes. Bernini worked in Rome for most of his life and one of his patrons, Pope Urban VIII, claimed that *"Bernini was made for Rome and Rome was made for Bernini."*

Portraits

Photography was not invented until the nineteenth century. During the centuries before photography people depended on painters and sculptors to provide them with images of themselves. Bernini created a new and **spontaneous** type of portrait bust. Bernini began by making sketches on paper of the sitter. He then made a small-scale bozzetto (see box on page 37). This early stage was essential for Bernini because it helped him to plan the composition of the bust and to get to know the sitter. When Bernini finally came to carve the marble he was able to capture the face of his sitter as if it had been caught in the middle of a conversation. The eyes Bernini carved seem to be clues to the personalities of the people he sculpted—he carefully drilled the hole of an eye's pupil so that it appeared alive. Coils of hair and lacy collars were also delicately drilled into the marble so that they looked realistic. Bernini sculpted as if his tools were really paintbrushes and he were painting on canvas, not cutting hard and difficult marble.

Playing to an Audience

Bernini sculpted four life-sized mythological statues for Cardinal Scipione Borghese. These sculptures each show a scene suddenly stopped in time. Unlike Benvenuto Cellini, Bernini wanted people to look at his sculptures from only one viewpoint and so every statue he made was intended to sit in a specific place in a room, chapel, stairway, or fountain. Bernini even added sculpted rays of sunlight to some of his works (see *The Ecstasy of St. Teresa,* left) so that it was obvious which direction people were supposed to view the sculptures from.

Bernini used special effects to illustrate this particular moment. Teresa, a Spanish nun born in 1515, claimed that her heart had been pierced with heavenly love by an angel.

The Ecstasy of St. Teresa, 1645–52.

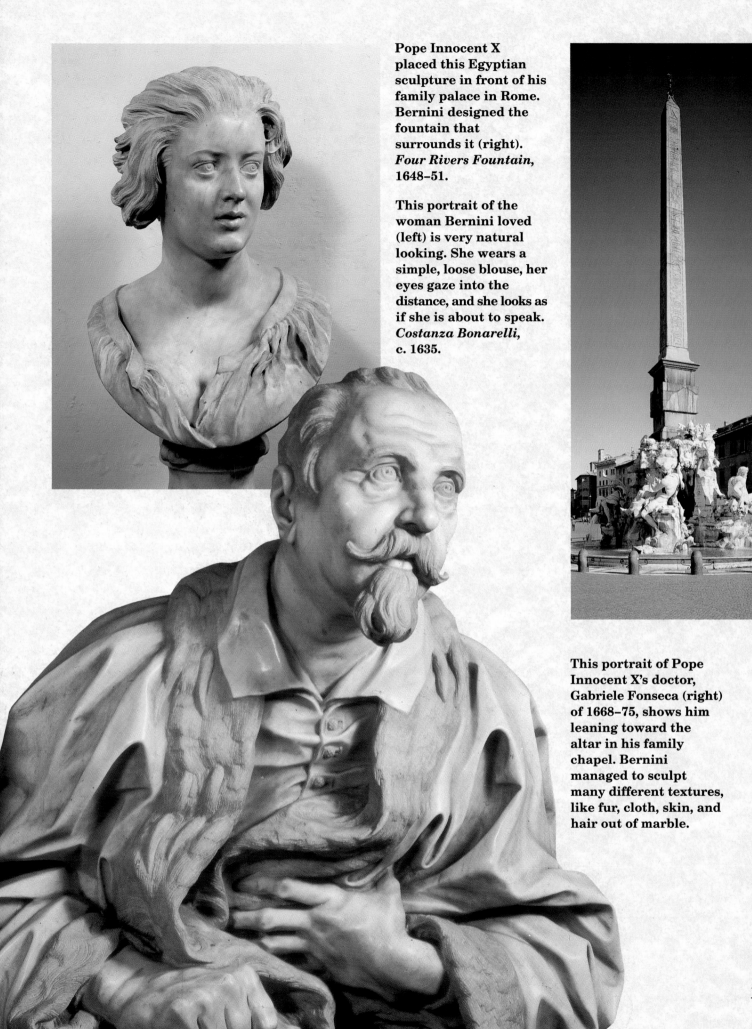

Pope Innocent X placed this Egyptian sculpture in front of his family palace in Rome. Bernini designed the fountain that surrounds it (right). *Four Rivers Fountain,* 1648–51.

This portrait of the woman Bernini loved (left) is very natural looking. She wears a simple, loose blouse, her eyes gaze into the distance, and she looks as if she is about to speak. *Costanza Bonarelli,* c. 1635.

This portrait of Pope Innocent X's doctor, Gabriele Fonseca (right) of 1668–75, shows him leaning toward the altar in his family chapel. Bernini managed to sculpt many different textures, like fur, cloth, skin, and hair out of marble.

39

The unknown Roman sculptor who created this bust of Plato imagined what he might have looked like. c. first century A.D.

5: CLASSIC IDEAS

Academies

Artists had become very influential members of society—Bernini and the painter **Rubens** (1577–1640) were welcomed in European courts as honored guests. More and more people were attracted to the artistic professions. Academies, or schools, were set up in Europe to train these artists properly.

Learning to Sculpt

Academies were not a new invention—the first academy was established by the Greek **philosopher Plato** in about 387 B.C. Plato held classes in an olive grove outside Athens. From this time onward the name "academy" was given to any group of people interested in meeting to talk about philosophy or literature.

During the Renaissance, art was often a subject of debate. Lorenzo de' Medici encouraged artists to visit and discuss his collection of paintings and sculptures. Cosimo de' Medici founded an academy of design with Michelangelo and himself at its head.

In 1648 Louis XIV of France founded an academy in Paris to give artists a practical training. This academy became the forerunner of over a hundred academies that were set up all over Europe by the eighteenth century.

Artists were taught to follow a definite set of artistic rules. These rules were usually influenced by the popular tastes and fashions of the time. To enter an academy you had to submit one of your works, which was then judged by a special jury of teachers. If your work was thought to be good enough then you were allowed to become a member of the academy.

Copying the Past

Once an artist had entered an academy he was taught by artists who were considered to be masters in their fields. Copying Classical Greek and Roman sculpture (see pages 6–13) was considered the best training for any apprentice sculptor. But it was not possible for everyone to travel to Rome or Athens so plaster casts were made of the original works and sent all over Europe. Academies collected as many casts as possible to provide their students with useful examples of work to learn from.

Casts used by students are often part of public collections. This nineteenth-century painting of a Russian art academy (background) shows casts of many Greek and Roman sculptures, such as *Laocoön* and *Venus de Milo* (see page 7).

These two mythological figures examine a large butterfly.
Antonio Canova, *Love and Psyche*, 1793.

Neoclassicism

By the middle of the eighteenth century many philosophers, writers, artists and politicians thought that the best way forward for mankind was through science and **rational** thought. This movement was called the **Enlightenment** and its influence can be seen in Neoclassical art. Neoclassical artists returned to the simplicity of the work of Ancient Greek and Roman sculptors. This style of art and architecture tried to recreate the heroic art of the Greeks and Romans as a way of inspiring people with a new feeling of **civic pride**.

Canova

Antonio Canova (1757–1822) was an Italian sculptor who became director of Rome's academy. Canova always used pure white marble to sculpt his simple, beautiful, images. Canova was the most influential Neoclassical sculptor of his day and worked for **Napoleon**, the **Duke of Wellington** and **Catherine the Great**.

This beautiful statue depicts two mythological figures and tries to explain the idea that love awakens the mind and soul.
Antonio Canova, *Cupid and Psyche*, 1787–93.

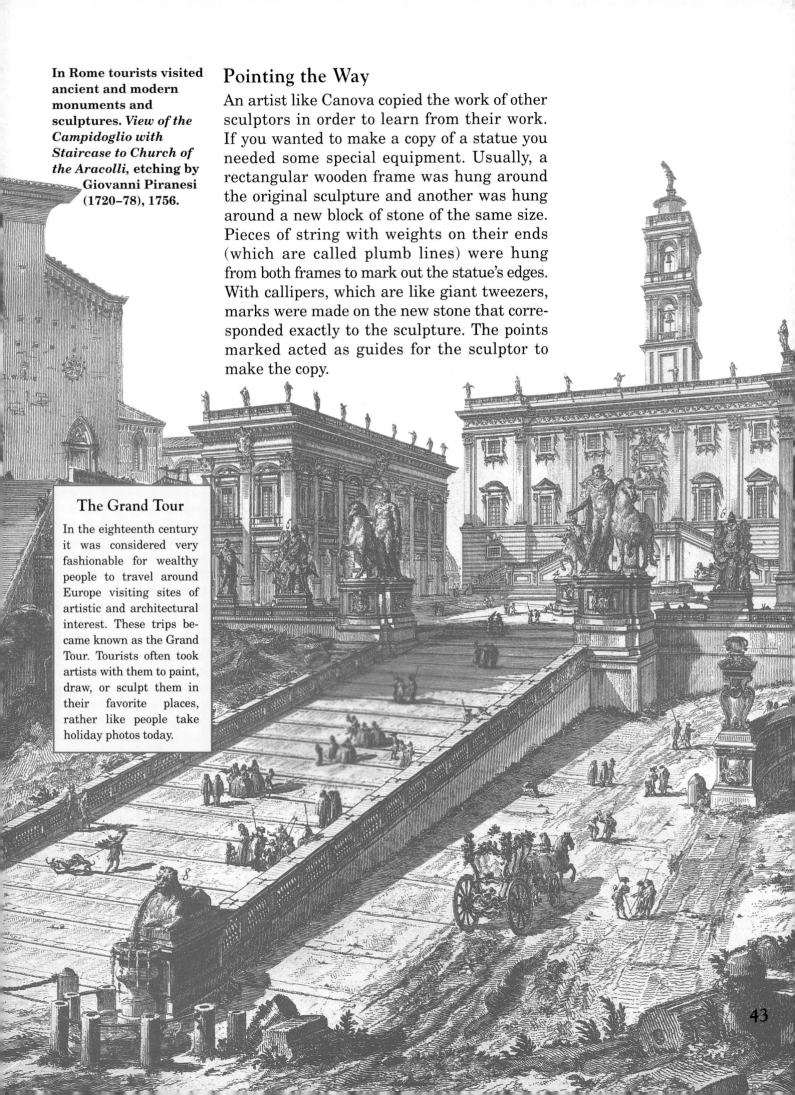

In Rome tourists visited ancient and modern monuments and sculptures. *View of the Campidoglio with Staircase to Church of the Aracolli*, etching by Giovanni Piranesi (1720–78), 1756.

Pointing the Way

An artist like Canova copied the work of other sculptors in order to learn from their work. If you wanted to make a copy of a statue you needed some special equipment. Usually, a rectangular wooden frame was hung around the original sculpture and another was hung around a new block of stone of the same size. Pieces of string with weights on their ends (which are called plumb lines) were hung from both frames to mark out the statue's edges. With callipers, which are like giant tweezers, marks were made on the new stone that corresponded exactly to the sculpture. The points marked acted as guides for the sculptor to make the copy.

The Grand Tour

In the eighteenth century it was considered very fashionable for wealthy people to travel around Europe visiting sites of artistic and architectural interest. These trips became known as the Grand Tour. Tourists often took artists with them to paint, draw, or sculpt them in their favorite places, rather like people take holiday photos today.

43

6: FRANCE IN THE NINETEENTH CENTURY

The French objected to the luxurious lifestyle of their king (above) and queen. Antoine P. Callet, *Louis XVI,* before 1786.
The Execution of Queen Marie-Antoinette (above right), painted in the eighteenth century by an unknown Dutch artist.

The Arc de Triomphe has several surfaces where sculptures illustrate republican ideas.

Revolution

In 1789 the people of France revolted against the government of their king and queen, Louis XVI and Marie Antoinette, and declared their country a **republic.** For a long time after the Revolution, French art depicted popular war images. Some of the greatest "Revolutionary" pictures were painted by artists who, at the time of the Revolution were only small children.

Inspiring Sculptures

The painting *Liberty Leading the People* (1830) by **Eugène Delacroix** (1798–1863) depicts the spirit of the French people during the revolution of 1830 as they join to fight against King Charles X. The *Departure of the Volunteers in 1792* (opposite page) by François Rude (1784–1855) was made five years after Delacroix's painting and shows soldiers being encouraged to fight by the main figure who represents the French nation. This sculpture was designed for the **Arc de Triomphe,** which is a triumphal arch that can still be seen in Paris. This arch served the same purpose as the triumphal arches that were made by the Romans (see pages 12–13).

Art that is erected in public places is intended to influence as many people as possible. Throughout the nineteenth century public monuments (nearly always sculptures) became more and more popular.

Every element of this relief encourages the person looking at it to be emotionally stirred. Figures, more like classical soldiers than French people of the time, move with great energy or remain thoughtful. François Rude, *The Departure of the Volunteers in 1792*, 1835–36.

A lively, joyful group of figures decorates the Opera building in Paris, Jean-Baptiste Carpeaux, *The Dance*, 1867–69.

A Changing Style

The years following the Revolution of 1789 were not peaceful. The Revolution had a great impact on the lives of the French people and many philosophers, poets, and artists wrote and painted about their experiences. Romanticism was the style that developed during this period (the turn of the eighteenth and nineteenth centuries). Romanticisim is a style that tries to express people's inner emotions. Many artists changed the working methods they had learned at their academies. Painters started to use brighter colors and to paint with broad brushstrokes. Sculptors began to leave the surfaces of their work rough and unfinished. Jean-Baptiste Carpeaux (1827–75) was a pupil of Rude and the figures in his most famous work, *The Dance* (above right), are lively and energetic. The subject matter of sculpture no longer had to be a scene from the past, the Bible, or mythology – ordinary people were as good a subject as Ancient gods.

45

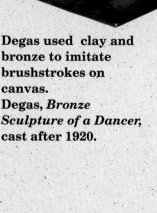

Painters and Sculptors

In his paintings Renoir created delicate flowers and light effects. **Auguste Renoir**, *On the Terrace*, 1881.

Quite often, painters, sculptors, writers, and musicians share many of the same ideas. Painters and sculptors discuss their art and meet to exchange their views. Some painters turn to sculpture and some sculptors turn to painting in order to express their ideas.

The Impressionists

A group of painters working mostly in Paris from the 1860s onward became interested in the way our eyes see things and how different light affects our vision. These painters were named the Impressionists because some of their paintings were more like quick impressions of what they saw rather than traditional, detailed studies.

Degas and Renoir

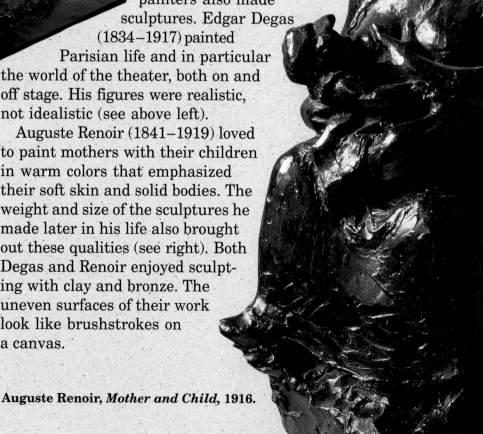

Some Impressionist painters also made sculptures. Edgar Degas (1834–1917) painted Parisian life and in particular the world of the theater, both on and off stage. His figures were realistic, not idealistic (see above left).

Auguste Renoir (1841–1919) loved to paint mothers with their children in warm colors that emphasized their soft skin and solid bodies. The weight and size of the sculptures he made later in his life also brought out these qualities (see right). Both Degas and Renoir enjoyed sculpting with clay and bronze. The uneven surfaces of their work look like brushstrokes on a canvas.

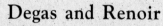

Degas used clay and bronze to imitate brushstrokes on canvas.
Degas, *Bronze Sculpture of a Dancer,* **cast after 1920.**

46

Auguste Renoir, *Mother and Child,* **1916.**

The Maori people of Polynesia carved striking images of faces and figures to represent their ancestry and beliefs (above). Maori wood carving from New Zealand.

Gauguin admired the simple style of Polynesian sculpture. He adapted this style to illustrate ideas that often related to his earlier life in France (right). Paul Gauguin, *Religious Panel*, c. 1889.

A Postimpressionist Sculptor

Paul Gauguin (1848–1903) was one of the first artists of the generation that followed the Impressionists. Gauguin was greatly influenced by the work of the Impressionists but developed his own style and became part of the **Postimpressionist** movement. Gauguin was attracted to a more simple life than the one he found in Paris and in 1891 he traveled to Tahiti (in French Polynesia) where he produced some of his finest work. Much of Gauguin's work was inspired by the bold and simple wood carvings of the South Pacific people and his sculptures resemble these Polynesian carvings.

It took Rodin eighteen months to create this statue. Rodin used a Belgian soldier as his model.
The Age of Bronze, 1876.

In *Love Fleeing* of 1881, Rodin managed to capture a feeling of movement between two figures cast in bronze.

Rodin

The Impressionist painters were not admired or appreciated at first. One criticism of their work was that the subjects they chose – ordinary town and country life – were not suitable subject matter for art. Auguste Rodin (1840–1917) was a sculptor living in Paris at the same time as the Impressionists. His work was also disliked at first but he is now thought of as the genius of nineteenth-century sculpture.

Frozen in Time

When Rodin's statue *The Age of Bronze* (right) was first shown to the public (in 1877), people thought that it had been cast from real life because it was so lifelike. Rodin watched people very closely to note how their bodies moved. From photographs you can see a movement frozen in an instant. Sculpture also shows someone or something at one particular moment in time – Rodin chose the moment his sculpture was to depict very carefully.

48

Camille Claudel (1864–1943)

Camille Claudel became a pupil of Rodin's in 1884. It was very unusual at this time for a woman to be a sculptor – sculpture was not considered a suitable occupation for a woman. Camille helped Rodin by posing as a model and assisting him in the final stages of modeling and casting his work. But Claudel was also a very talented sculptor in her own right and was an expert in the use of both bronze and marble. Many of Claudel's works are portraits of her family, characters from mythology, and dancers.

The Burghers of Calais

The Burghers of Calais (above, 1885–95) is a public monument. Rodin chose to tell the story of an incident that took place in the French seaside town of Calais in 1347. Six noblemen were taken hostage and then forced by the English to leave Calais in humiliation. The noblemen also had to surrender the keys of the town to the English. At first, Rodin sculpted each figure naked so that he could show the movements of their bodies accurately. Once he had mastered their figures Rodin put their clothes back on. Each person seems to suffer alone and yet all the figures follow each other in a slow, sad, circular walk.

Bumpy Sculptures

Like the Impressionists, much of Rodin's success came when people appreciated the way he used his materials. Sometimes Rodin deliberately left the stone, plaster, or bronze, rough—rather like the Impressionists' brushstrokes. Because Rodin's sculptures are not smooth, they seem unfinished, but an uneven surface catches the light and can make the work look more lively and interesting.

The six men cannot be seen together from any one angle of this sculpture. They appear to be part of an ever-changing, moving group.
The Burghers of Calais, (1885–95).

Rodin created statues of famous people showing them as individuals. The public was shocked to see the great French novelist Honoré de Balzac (1799–1850) wearing a coat like a dressing gown.
Balzac, 1897.

7: THE TWENTIETH CENTURY

Changing Forms

Looking back over the last hundred years we can see that the twentieth century has been a time of fast-moving change. Art is like a reflection of life – world events, or the artist's feelings about world events, are often depicted in art. From the time of the Impressionists onward (see pages 46–47) artists broke with the traditions of the past and the purpose of art changed – **avant-garde** art was born.

Between Rodin and the Modern Age

Aristide Maillol (1861–1944) concentrated on sculpting one subject his entire life – the female nude. Unlike Rodin, Maillol produced plain shapes in simple poses that express emotion from within. Maillol's nudes are grand and timeless and unconnected to historical or mythological subjects even though he studied Ancient Greek and Roman sculptures (see pages 6–13).

Sculpting Speed

The Futurists were a group of Italian artists who believed that painters had to make a complete break with the artistic traditions of the past and that the modern world of machines was more important than anything else. The Futurists tried to depict emotional new experiences like speeding along on motorcycles. They published statements, called manifestos, to make people understand their views on the excitement of machines and the new century.

Aristide Maillol captured the moment these figures (above and below) appear surprised into action.

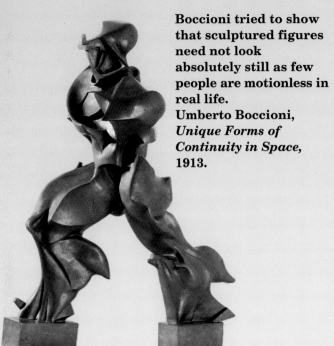

Umberto Boccioni (1882–1916) was a Futurist painter and (the only) Futurist sculptor. Boccioni's sculptures are of running figures that look shattered and fragmented because they are moving so fast that we cannot see them properly. Boccioni believed that glass, electric lights, and electric motors should be used to create movement in sculptures, but unfortunately he died in an accident during World War I (1914–18) before he could put any of his ideas to the test.

Abstraction

In the early twentieth century artists became less concerned with painting and sculpting recognizable people, events, or objects and more interested in making abstract art. An abstract work of art is one which does not have a readily recognizable subject.

Constantin Brancusi (1876–1957) once had his sculpture, *Bird in Space,* refused by a **customs official** who said it was not a work of art but a piece of metal. Brancusi had reduced the bird's recognizable parts, like feathers, claws, and beak, to a simple shape because he wanted to draw attention to the beauty of the material.

Jean Arp (1887–1966) was also interested in sculpting the shapes he saw in nature. Arp's works look like plants or animals and yet they do not imitate them perfectly like photographs.

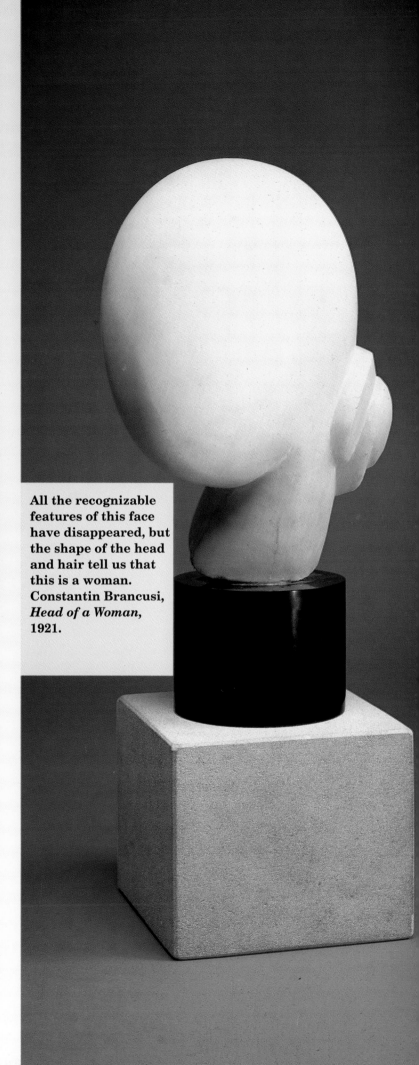

Objects of Art

There had always been two main methods of sculpting – either to carve, taking away pieces of material, like marble, or to model and add material like clay. Sculptors often discussed these working methods and during the early decades of the twentieth century a third method was created – using objects as sculpture or as parts of sculpture.

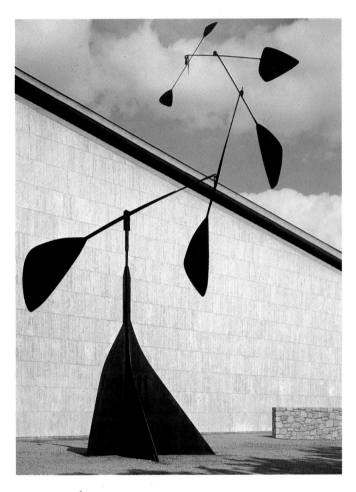

Picasso's Sculptures

The painter **Pablo Picasso** (1881–1973) combined paint and collage and stuck paper and cloth onto painted surfaces. Picasso's experiments varied and progressed and soon he was creating reliefs and sculptures made up of objects like scrap metal. Picasso made sculptures out of objects like bicycle handlebars and old bottles. Like Gauguin (see page 47), Picasso was influenced by the sculpture of other cultures, especially African tribal works, which were only just being brought back to Paris by explorers, writers, and collectors.

52

Inventing the Mobile

The American sculptor and painter Alexander Calder (1898–1976) became famous in both Europe and America in the 1930s for his portraits made out of wire and his abstract drawings.

Calder marked out pin-points in space using wire and metal which he painted. In 1932 Marcel Duchamp named one of Calder's wire sculptures a mobile – sculpture suspended in the air that moves freely. Calder has been remembered as the inventor of the mobile ever since.

Alexander Calder's *Useless Machine* (left).

Ready-made Sculptures

During World War I (1914–18) people were shocked into thinking that life had little meaning. Some artists believed that art should reflect this attitude. Why couldn't all objects, even a pile of rubbish, be called "art"?

Marcel Duchamp (1887–1968) invented "ready-made" sculpture which was not really created sculptures but objects selected and assembled by the sculptor. Duchamp delcared that a bicycle wheel stuck on a kitchen stool was art.

Looking carefully at this imposing figure (right) you can recognize individual objects and see how they are all welded together. Pablo Picasso, *La Tailiere*.

The Constructivists

In about 1913 the Russian Vladimir Tatlin (1885–1953) founded the art movement Constructivism. Along with the brothers Antoine Pevsner (1886–1962) and Naum Gabo (1890–1977) who were both artists and sculptors, Tatlin made paintings, architecture, and sculpture that was "constructed." Tatlin made abstract constructions of wood, metal, and glass that he put together like machines instead of modeling or carving. These were materials that people could recognize from everyday life, unlike marble or bronze.

Naum Gabo used modern materials, like transparent plastic and glass, in his work as a way of challenging old ideas of "art." You can see through some of Gabo's sculptures and the shapes made by the plastic seem strange as if they aren't really there at all. Gabo also made sculptures out of paper and cardboard and set them in a frame that made them look as though they were peeking out from the corner of a room.

Tatlin's *Monument to the Third International,* a tower of steel, wood, and glass, was originally made in 1919 and has since been destroyed. This copy was made in the 1970s in London.

This sculpture (left) has been built up out of sheets of metal to represent a head, shoulders, and hands. Naum Gabo, *Head no. 2,* 1916.

53

War and Peace

Wars have been fought throughout history and many wars have been commemorated with public works of sculpture.

The Statue of Liberty

One of the world's most famous statues was inspired by a war—the American War of Independence (1775–83). We have to step back in time to the nineteenth century to discover its history.

In 1865 a young French sculptor, Frédéric Bartholdi (1834–1904), was having dinner near Paris when the idea of a monument to American independence was discussed. Bartholdi never forgot this idea and soon sailed to New York to seek American support for the project. In 1875 Bartholdi's first clay model was about five feet high and this was replaced by another model thirty-eight feet high. As each part of the copper statue was completed, Parisians made excursions to take a look at its progress. Before the statue was shipped to New York, builders in America made a pedestal from the largest amount of concrete ever poured —23,000 tons.

Liberty now stands in New York harbor where millions of people since Bartholdi have had their first view of America. *Liberty* is over one hundred sixty-five feet high and her nose alone is five feet long.

A view of the top of the *Statue of Liberty*.

The Statue of Liberty **seen from the air is an impressive sight her creator could never have imagined.**

War Memorials

All over the world, people who fought and died in wars are remembered in monuments that are in the streets and churches of their hometowns or villages. Their names, or a dedication to them, are inscribed on sculptures that include images of soldiers, guns, death, peace, and freedom. Sometimes the metal used on these memorials has been taken from guns retrieved from the battlefield. Unlike triumphal arches or columns (see pages 12–13), war memorials do not celebrate success, but act as reminders to the living of those who have died.

This war memorial at Verdun in France (below left) was built from 1928–32 in memory of the soldiers who died there in 1916 during World War I (1914–18).

The Marine Corps War Memorial in the national cemetery at Arlington, Virginia, by Felix W. de Weldon (below right). It shows the raising of the flag on Iwo Jima in World War II. It honors all marines who have died for their country.

Politics and Art

The **Communist** politician and **theorist** Vladimir Ilyich Lenin once declared that *"art belongs to the People."* With his minister of education, Lenin encouraged the policy of "Agitprop." Agitprop was the name given to the **propaganda** that was communicated to the people of the new Soviet Republic through public works of art—especially through sculpture. Both **Adolf Hitler** and **Benito Mussolini**, the World War II (1939–45) German and Italian dictators, used painting, architecture, and sculpture as a way of promoting their policies.

Hitler used theater and art as propaganda. This is one of his political meetings.

NAVAL·WAR·1798–1801×TRIPOLI·1801–1805×·WAR·OF·1812–1815 × FLORIDA·INDIAN·WARS·1835–1842× MEXICO·1846–1848

Yesterday, Today, and Tomorrow

The social, political, and technological changes that have taken place throughout the twentieth century have produced many artists with their own individual styles and subject matter. Sculptors in the past usually conformed to the wishes of their patrons and the fashions of their time. Artists today have much more freedom to pursue their own ideas. After World War II, two sculptors in particular,

Henry Moore (1898–1986) and Alberto Giacometti (1901–66), stood out as having their own distinctive styles. These artists were not associated with any particular group of artists for any significant amount of time.

Light falls, creating new shapes and emphasizing the bronze surface of this study by Henry Moore. *Reclining Figure no. 2,* **1963.**

Alberto Giacometti, *Man Pointing,* **1947.**

Henry Moore

As a young man the British sculptor Henry Moore studied the art of primitive cultures in the British Museum and was very influenced by its simplicity and shape. In his sculpture, Moore wanted to depict human feelings in natural shapes and declared that he *"always paid attention to natural forms such as bones, shells, and pebbles."* Moore admired the work of Michelangelo and, like Michelangelo, had a long and successful career. Moore sculpted with traditional materials, like stone and bronze, but his figures are continuous natural shapes, as if they were joined together. One of Moore's favorite subjects was the family, or a mother with her child. These groups are large, carved, solid masses that almost look abstract. Moore, like Brancusi (see pages 50–51), wanted the beauty of the material he was using to be one of the main features of the work.

Alberto Giacometti

Alberto Giacometti was a Swiss sculptor who began his career as a **Surrealist** and then returned to making more natural-looking sculptures. Giacometti's figures became smaller and smaller and thinner and thinner the longer he worked on them. Giacometti chose to make spaces an important part of his work. He left distances between his skeletonlike figures to make them seem lost and lonely in the modern world.

Inside Museums

Sculpture can be found all around us, in the street, in the classroom—but most of all in museums. A great deal of sculpture is kept in museums under the correct conditions in order to ensure its protection. We can return again and again to a museum to see fragments of a Greek frieze where its carving can be studied close at hand. But during the thousands of years that sculpture has been made, it was rarely planned to be seen in a museum.

Sculpture Installations

Today, some sculptors design their work specifically for museums. These sculptures are not always a single piece of work, but whole rooms arranged so that people can walk into them and experience the atmosphere that the artist has created. These arrangements of materials and sculptures are called "installations."

**This sculpture rises from the water enlivened by patches of color (left).
Joan Miró (1893–1983), *Woman and Bird*, 1981–82.**

Christo (b. 1935) is known as the inventor of "packaging" art—wrapping up familiar objects in plastic or canvas. Christo surrounded many islands in Biscayne Bay, Florida, with pink plastic in 1983. *Pink Island.*

A Sculpture or a Pile of Bricks?

Carl Andre (b. 1935) arranged one hundred and twenty bricks in a long rectangle on the floor of the Tate Gallery in London. Andre called these bricks *Equivalent VIII* (see below). The bricks depended on careful positioning in the gallery to make them into an artwork because if they had just been lying around on a building site no one would have taken any notice of them. There was a public outcry against this sculpture and it was **vandalized** in 1976. Many people refused to think of *Equivalent VIII* as a work of art – others argued it was.

The Sculpture of Tomorrow

The many purposes of sculpture have changed a great deal over thousands of years. Sculptors are now expected to think up newer and newer ideas whereas a thousand years ago they were expected to sculpt in the exact way that they had been taught by their master. A stonemason from the Middle Ages would be puzzled to see a pile of bricks called sculpture but he would also be amazed to see the angel he had carved on the door of a cathedral standing inside a glass cabinet in a museum. Like the stonemason, we shall all just have to imagine what kind of sculpture will be sitting in art galleries in a thousand years' time.

Andy Goldsworthy (b. 1956) is another British sculptor who uses nature for both his subject and as his materials. *Sticks and Stones,* **Central Park, New York City, 1993.**

Art Outside Museums

Some modern sculptors do not want their work to be preserved. Art has always imitated the real world but nowadays we are very aware of how nature is threatened by the way we live. Many sculptors regard nature itself as a work of art with the whole world as a museum.

Robert Smithson (1938–1973) built a jetty from the shore of the Great Salt Lake in Utah. He knew the water would alter its appearance and eventually wear it down, and this element of change is what he wanted to include in his sculpture. The jetty is now under the water.

Carl Andre's *Equivalent VIII* **of 1966. Do you think this is "art" or just a pile of bricks?**

Glossary

A

abrasive: something that is used to wear away, remove, or smooth down a rough surface is called an abrasive.

anonymous: when a work of art is called anonymous it means that we do not know who created it.

Apollo: the Ancient Greek god of sun, music, poetry, farming, country life, and prophecy.

Arc de Triomphe: a triumphal arch that **Napoleon** began building in 1806 to **commemorate** his military victories of 1805–06. The Arc was completed in 1836 and stands in the Place de L'Etoile in Paris.

Athena: the Greek goddess of war, the arts and crafts, and wisdom.

avant-garde: a term that was used after the French Revolution to describe any revolutionary political movement. The term avant-garde began to be used at the beginning of this century to describe artists who made art that differed from the teaching of the academies.

B

b.: born, followed by date.

baptistery: a small chapel used for weddings and christenings, usually next to a cathedral.

Barbarians: the name given by the Ancient Greeks and Romans to foreign peoples. After the fall of the Roman Empire, Barbarians moved and settled all over Europe.

bust: a sculpture of a person's head and shoulders.

C

c.: circa, or approximately, usually used with a date.

Catherine the Great: Catherine II (1729–96) became empress of Russia in 1762. Catherine was a **patron** of the arts and expanded Russia's empire as far as Turkey and Poland.

city-state: a city with its own laws, government, and (sometimes) army.

civic pride: a pride in the town or city in which you live.

colossal: huge.

commemorative: a piece of writing, sculpture, music, or art that is created as a tribute to a person or many people who have died.

communism: politics based on the writings of the German philosophers Karl Marx (1818–83) and Friedrich Engels (1820–95). The first country to adopt communism as its form of government was Russia in 1917. In this system goods are supposed to be owned in common and used by anyone as needed.

composition: the name given to the way the elements of a painting or sculpture are arranged by the artist.

customs official: someone who is responsible for checking the entry of people and goods into his or her country.

D

d.: died, followed by a date.

dedicated: devoted to.

Delacroix, Eugène: (1798–1863) one of the greatest Romantic painters.

diameter: the measurement of the straight line that can be drawn through a circle from its center to its edges.

Duke of Wellington: Arthur Wellesley (1769–1852) was the first duke of Wellington. Wellington defeated **Napoleon** at the battle of Waterloo in 1815. He was also prime minister of Britain from 1828 to 1830.

E

engraver: someone who engraves. Engraving involves cutting a drawing or design into a block of wood or metal. Ink or paint is then applied to the block and the image is pressed onto a piece of paper.

Enlightenment: a European intellectual movement of the eighteenth century. The thinkers of the Enlightenment believed that society should be governed according to **rational** thought.

equestrian: anything do do with horses.

F

formal: in art, an image that is structured according to a set of artistic rules (or a style).

freestanding: something that is not attached to anything for support.

frieze: an area given over to the telling of a story in pictures or sculptures on or inside a building.

G

genius: someone who is born with a special talent and is more gifted than almost anyone else in a particular skill.

ground: a substance, such as powdered chalk, that is put onto a surface, such as wood, to protect it when paint is applied to it.

H

Hitler, Adolf: (1889–1945) leader of the German Nazi Party from 1921–45. Head of the German state from 1934–45. Hitler created a dictatorship and began a policy of claiming land as German. This policy led to the invasion of Poland in 1939, France and Great Britain's declaration of war on Germany, and World War II.

I

ideal: when something (such as a sculpted face) is called ideal it means that it is considered to be perfect.

incise: to cut into.

Iron Age: the name given to the time when tools and weapons were made out of iron. Archaeologists think that the Iron Age began in Thailand in c. 1600 B.C.

L

lacework: any drawing, sculpture, or painting that imitates the look and intricate design of lace.

Latin: a language of Ancient Italy that was spoken by educated people throughout the Roman Empire. Latin was the language of learning during the Middle Ages and the Renaissance.

Lent: for Christians, the forty days of fasting that come before Easter every year. Lent begins on Ash Wednesday and does not include the Sundays of the forty day period.

lodge: a small hut or house used for shelter, storage, eating, and as a meeting place.

M

magistrates: legal representatives who attend local courts in order to prosecute minor crimes.

mason: a workman who is skilled in cutting stone and constructing stone buildings.

master-mason: a **mason** who is more experienced and skilled than any other. A master-mason teaches and directs the work of the masons under his control.

Medici: the banking and merchant family that ruled Florence from 1437–1737. The Medici were important **patrons** of the arts.

Mediterranean: the inland sea between Europe and North Africa.

Medusa: Medusa was a woman from Greek **mythology** who was turned into a gorgon, a beast with wings, claws, and snakes for hair.

Mussolini, Benito : (1883–1945) founder of the Italian Fascist movement and dictator of Italy from 1922–43. Mussolini supported **Adolf Hitler** in World War II.

mythological: to do with stories of gods, goddesses, heroes, and heroines.

N

Napoleon: (1769–1821) in 1799 Napoleon Bonaparte overthrew the French government and made himself the ruler of France (1804–14 and 1814–15). Napoleon conquered most of Europe but was eventually forced to give up power in 1814 and was sent into exile on the island of Elba. After regaining power later in 1814 Napoleon was finally defeated at the Battle of Waterloo (see **Duke of Wellington**).

Netherlands: a name for modern-day Holland.

niche: a hollow in a wall.

O

Old Testament: the first of the two major parts of the Bible.

P

Parthenon: the temple of **Athena** on the hill of the Acropolis in Athens. The Parthenon was built from 477–432 B.C. and is the finest surviving example of Greek architecture and sculpture.

patron: someone who supports the arts by paying artists and sculptors to work for him or her.

persecuted: to be persecuted is to be hunted down and punished for what you believe in (usually for religious or political reasons).

Perseus: a Greek god who was the son of **Zeus** and killed **Medusa**.

Persia: a powerful nation of southwest Asia that ruled the Ancient world until c. A.D. 331. Persia was in modern-day Iran.

philosopher: someone who thinks about the things that govern our lives for which we have no scientific answers, such as the existence of God.

Picasso, Pablo: (1881–1973) the most famous artist of this century. Picasso was Spanish and is associated with the **avant-garde.**

pilgrimage: a journey, made as an act of religious devotion, to a sacred place.

plague: a disease transmitted by rats that wiped out a large number of people during the Middle Ages.

Plato: (c. 428–347 B.C.) Greek **philosopher** who wrote many philosophical dialogues and founded an academy (see pages 40–41).

portable: something that is small enough to be carried.

Postimpressionist: the group of artists who came after the Impressionists. Vincent van Gogh, Paul Cézanne, and Paul Gauguin were Postimpressionists.

propaganda: information distributed by governments or individuals that is designed to form the opinions of the people for whom it is intended.

prophet: an inspired religious teacher or preacher who foretells religious happenings.

pulpit: a platform or structure used for preaching from.

pumice stone: a stone formed from volcanic eruptions and used for cleaning or smoothing.

R

rational: anything that is sensible, intelligent, or reasonable.

realistic: anything that resembles real things.

renaissance: a rebirth of interest and activity in a subject area such as painting, sculpture, or literature.

republic: an independent country that has no monarch and is ruled by an elected government.

Rubens, Peter Paul: (1577–1640) a painter from Flanders (modern-day Holland and Belgium) who was a court painter and the leading figure of Baroque art. The Baroque style began in Italy and spread all over Europe. Baroque artists were concerned with balance and harmony in their compositions and subject matter. Bernini was a Baroque sculptor (see pages 38–39).

S

sanctuary: the name given to the most holy part of a temple or church.

sarcophagus: a type of coffin used by the Ancient Greeks and Romans. A sarcophagus was usually made of limestone.

senator: a member of the senate of Ancient Rome. The senate governed Ancient Rome and so a senator was like a modern-day member of Congress.

spontaneous: to do something on impulse is to act in a spontaneous way.

Surrealism

Surrealism: a type of art that started in France in the 1920s. Surrealism spread all over Europe, especially into Germany and Spain. The Surrealists tried to paint the unknown world of the mind, dreams, and the irrational (the opposite of **rational**).

symbol: an emblem or image that represents something other than itself.

symbolic: something that is represented by **symbols** and so represents something other than itself (see box on page 13).

synthetic: produced artificially.

T

technique: the process or practice that is used to obtain particular artistic effects.

theorist: someone who is concerned with constructing theories. A theory is an unproven idea or way of thinking about something.

translucent: something that can be partially seen through.

Trojan: someone from Troy. Troy was an ancient city of Asia Minor. The Trojans are most famous for their war with the Greeks in the mid-thirteenth century B.C.

V

vandalize: to harm or destroy something on purpose.

Z

Zeus: the chief of the Greek gods.

zinc: a substance that is part metal and is bluish-white in color. Zinc is used in paint, glass, brass, cosmetics, and printing ink.

Further Reading

Arenas, Jose F. *The Key to Renaissance Art.* Lerner, 1990

Cush, Cathie. *Artists Who Created Great Works,* "20 Events" series. Raintree Steck-Vaughn, 1995

Greenberg, Jan and Jordan, Sandra. *The Sculptor's Eye: Looking at Contemporary American Art.* Delacorte, 1993

Levine, Bobbie, et al. *A Child's Walk Through Twentieth Century American Painting and Sculpture.* University of Michigan, Museum of Art, 1986

Martin, Ana. *Romanesque Art and Architecture.* Childrens, 1993

McLanathan, Richard. *Michelangelo.* Abrams, 1993

Pekarik, Andrew. *Sculpture.* Hyperion Books for Children, 1992

Raboff, Ernest. *Michelangelo Buonarroti.* HarperCollins Children's, 1988

Index